SCIENCE

MAGIC

WITH LIGHT

CHRIS OXLADE

BARRON'S

First edition for the United States, Canada, and the Philippines published 1994 by Barron's Educational Series, Inc.

Design
David West Children's Book Design
Designer
Steve Woosnam-Savage
Editor
Suzanne Melia
Illustrator
Ian Thompson
Photographer
Roger Vlitos

© Aladdin Books Ltd. 1993
Created and designed by
N.W. Books
28 Percy Street
London W1P 9FF

First published in
Great Britain in 1993 by
Franklin Watts Ltd.
96 Leonard Street
London EC2A 4RH

All inquiries should be addressed to:
Barron's Educational Series, Inc.
250 Wireless Boulevard
Hauppauge, NY 11788

International Standard Book No.
0-8120-6445-3 (hardcover)
0-8120-1984-9 (paperback)

Library of Congress Catalog
Card No. 94-5549

Library of Congress Cataloging-in-Publication Data

Oxlade, Chris.
Science magic with light / Chris Oxlade. — 1st ed. for the U.S., Canada, and the Philippines.
p. cm. — (Science magic)
Includes index
ISBN 0-8120-6445-3. — ISBN 0-1820-1984-9 (pbk.).
1. Conjuring—Juvenile literature.
2. Light—Juvenile literature. 3. Scientific recreations—Juvenile literature. [1. Magic tricks. 2. Light. 3. Scientific recreations.]
I. Title. II. Series.
GV1548.096 1994   94-5549
793.8—dc20   CIP
                                                  AC

Printed in Belgium
4567 4208 987654321

CONTENTS

LIGHT MAGIC!

Most magic tricks would be pretty useless without light. Light enables us to see, and gives our world color. Light is amazingly versatile. It can pass straight through some substances, and causes ghostly reflections when it bounces off others. Light is a natural magician that can fool us into seeing things that just aren't there. Are they optical illusions or just tricks of the light?

BE AN EXPERT MAGICIAN

PREPARING YOUR ROUTINE

There is much more to being a magician than just doing tricks. It is important that you and your assistant practice your whole routine lots of times, so that your performance goes smoothly when you do it for an audience. You will be a more entertaining magician if you do.

PROPS

Props are all the bits and pieces of equipment that a magician uses during an act, including his or her clothes as well as the things needed for the tricks themselves. It's a good idea to make a magician's trunk from a large box to keep all your props in. During your routine, you can dip into the trunk, pulling out all sorts of equipment and crazy objects (see Misdirection). You could tell jokes about these objects.

PROPS LIST

Magic wand ★ Top hat Vest ★ Black marker pen Candle ★ Cardboard boxes ★ Cellophane tape Clear plastic or glass ★ Coins Colored paper for decorating or wrapping ★ Dowels ★ Eggs Flashlight ★ Food coloring ★ Glue Mirrors ★ Paints, some oil-based ★ Pencil Potted plant ★ Red and green cellophane Round plastic lid ★ Ruler ★ Scissors ★ Silk scarves or colored tissues ★ Tall glass ★ Thick cardboard ★ Thin cardboard, black and white ★ Thin wire ★ Water

WHICH TRICKS?

Work out which tricks you want to put in your routine. Include some long tricks and some short tricks.

WARNING: For one of the tricks in this book you need to light a candle. Be very careful that it does not set fire to anything.

MAGICIAN'S PATTER

Patter is what you say during your routine. Good patter makes a routine

much more interesting and allows it to run more smoothly. It is a good way to entertain your audience during the slower parts of your routine. Try to make up a story for each trick. Practice your patter when you practice your tricks.

MISDIRECTION

Misdirection is an important part of a magician's routine. By waving a colorful scarf in the air or telling a joke, you can distract an audience's attention from something you'd rather they didn't see!

KEEP IT SECRET

The best magicians never give away their secrets. If anyone asks how your tricks work, just reply, "By magic!" Then you can impress people with your tricks again and again.

INTRODUCING MAGIC MANDY
AND THE
VANISHING COIN

Magic Mandy makes the coin disappear with her amazing magic rings!

Ask to borrow a coin from the audience. Lay it on a piece of the patterned paper. Now put the white circle over the "spoof" ring and put the real ring on top. Pick up this pile and put it over the coin. Take off the real ring and white circle — the coin has disappeared! Put the circle and ring back and remove the pile. Suddenly the coin is back!

WHAT YOU NEED
Thin white cardboard
Scissors ★ Gold paint
Glue ★ Paper
(preferably wrapping paper with a random pattern) ★ Small coin

THE SCIENCE BEHIND THE TRICK

When the coin is covered by the ring with the patterned paper underneath it, the coin is hidden. But both rings look "see-through" to the audience when they are laid on the paper. The viewers think that they are seeing two distinct rings because they see what they think they should see! The ring hides the edge of the circle of patterned paper, which would give the secret away if it could be seen.

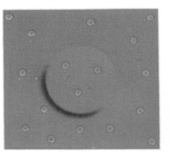

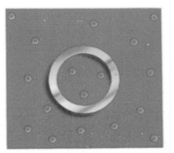

1 If you can't find wrapping paper
with a random pattern on it, paint a
random pattern on plain paper.

2 From the cardboard cut two rings
about 3 in. (8 cm) across
and paint them gold. Glue a
circle of the patterned paper
under one. Also cut out a
white cardboard
circle the same size as the rings.

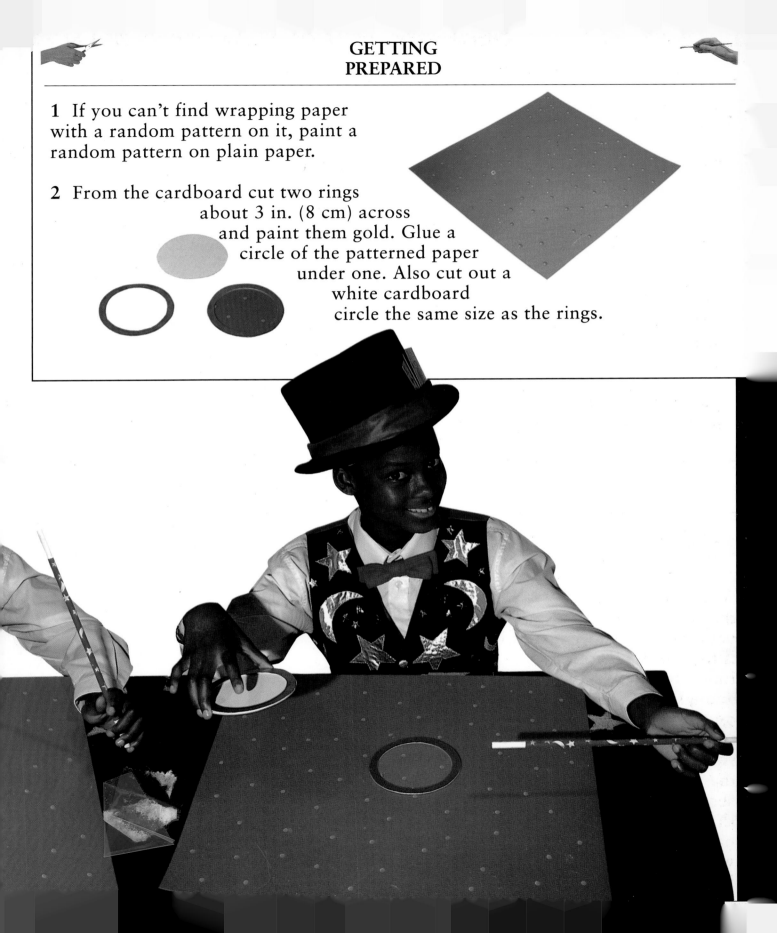

INTRODUCING MAGIC MEG
AND THE
GHOSTLY TUBE

The audience gasps as Magic Meg pulls scarves from the empty tube.

Before you start your act, put the silk scarves or tissue paper into the secret compartment. Hold the tube up to your audience so that they can see your face through it. This proves that the tube is empty. Now stand it up on the table with the secret compartment pointing upward. Produce the scarves with a flourish.

WHAT YOU NEED
Scissors ★ Thin cardboard ★ Cellophane tape ★ Glue ★ Colored paper or paints ★ Silk scarves or colored tissue paper

THE SCIENCE BEHIND THE TRICK

When you look along a long, straight road or railroad tracks, the sides of the road or the tracks seem to meet in the distance. This effect is called *linear perspective*, and we expect it to happen. When your audience looks through the ghostly tube, they think the sides look closer because of perspective, so they do not notice the secret compartment.

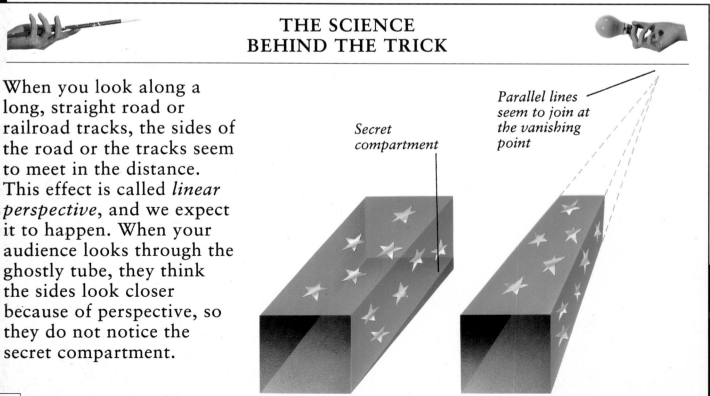

Secret compartment

Parallel lines seem to join at the vanishing point

GETTING PREPARED

1 Use the cardboard to make a tube about 4 in. (10 cm) square and 16 in. (40 cm) long. Glue another piece of cardboard inside to make a secret compartment.

2 Decorate the tube and stuff the compartment with scarves or tissue paper.

INTRODUCING MAGIC MEG
AND THE
AMAZING BLACK BOX

The audience gasps as Magic Meg pulls plants from thin air.

Before you start your act, load the plant into the black cylinder, and put the white cylinder and box over it. Lift out the white cylinder and show the audience that it is empty. Put it back and do the same with the box. Wave your wand and pull out the plant.

WHAT YOU NEED
Scissors ★ Thin cardboard (black and white) ★ Cellophane tape ★ Thick cardboard Colored paper or paints Potted plant

THE SCIENCE BEHIND THE TRICK

This trick works because the black cylinder blends in with the black inside the box. The bars help to hide the shape of the black cylinder. The audience thinks the box is empty. Magicians call this effect "black art." Because black doesn't reflect much light, it is hard to tell one area from another.

Black cylinder is hidden inside the white one

The black cylinder is difficult to see from the front and the box seems to be empty

1 Make a cylinder about 12 in. (30 cm) high and about 4.5 in. (12 cm) across out of the black cardboard. Make a white cylinder, slightly taller and wider than the black one, to fit over it.

2 Make a square box from the thick cardboard, the same height as the white cylinder and slightly wider, so that the white cylinder fits inside it. Cut a hole in the front and add bars as shown. Decorate the box.

WHAT YOU NEED
Rectangular mirror
Scissors ★ Thick
cardboard ★ Cellophane
tape ★ Colored paper or
paints ★ Silk scarves

For her next trick, Magic Mildred shows a box that is both empty and full!

Before you do the trick, load some silk scarves (or other objects) into the top of the box. Place the box on your table with the front flap pointing toward the audience. Open the front flap so that the audience can see inside. The box will look empty to them. Close it again, open the top flap, and produce the silk scarves.

THE SCIENCE BEHIND THE TRICK

The mirror inside the box must be at an angle of 45 degrees. When you look through the flap in the front of the box, you see the floor of the box and its reflection, in the mirror above it. The reflected floor looks like the back of the box.

Light

Mirror

14

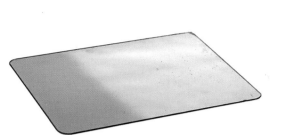

1 Measure the longer side of the mirror. Cut out two squares of cardboard with sides three-quarters of this length. These will be the sides of your box. Measure the shorter side of the mirror. This will be the width of your box.

2 Make up the box with the mirror inside it (the mirror goes from the front-top edge to the bottom-back edge at a 45-degree angle, with the mirrored side pointing down.) Cut flaps as shown, and decorate the box.

WHAT YOU NEED
Scissors ★ Thick white cardboard ★ Pencil Ruler ★ Black marker Sheet of black cardboard Two identical eggs

INTRODUCING MAGIC MARVIN
AND THE
ENLARGING TUNNEL

It's weird! As Magic Marvin moves the egg further away into the tunnel, the egg just gets bigger and bigger!

Make sure that you put the enlarging tunnel where the audience will be looking straight into it. Pick up your two eggs and place them in the tunnel, one near the front and the other near the back. Ask a volunteer which one is bigger. Now remove both eggs and give them to your volunteer, who will be amazed to find that they are the same size.

THE SCIENCE BEHIND THE TRICK

The enlarging tunnel works by tricking the eye — it's an optical illusion. We think that the far end of the tunnel looks smaller than the front because of perspective, and do not suspect that it actually is much smaller. This makes an object appear to get bigger as it moves further back into the tunnel. Quite the opposite to what we expect to see!

1 Cut this shape out of the thick cardboard: 20 in. (50 cm) long by 8 in. (20 cm) at the widest end.

2 Mark out the pattern with a pencil and ruler, and then color in the squares with the pen as shown. Make three more identical shapes and tape them together to form a tunnel.

3 Make a stand from the black cardboard, and cut a square opening in it. The larger end of the tunnel should fit into the hole.

INTRODUCING MAGIC MARCIA
AND THE
BENDING WIRE

What strange potion is it that bends solid wire for Magic Marcia?

Slide a piece of straight wire gradually into the potion — it will begin to look bent. Remove it and it's straight again! The second time, let the wire hit the bottom and keep pressing until it does bend. The audience will think the magic potion has bent it!

WHAT YOU NEED
Food coloring ★ *Tall glass of water* ★ *Thin wire (you should be able to bend it quite easily)* *Pliers*

THE SCIENCE BEHIND THE TRICK

When you put the wire into the water, it does not really bend; it just looks bent because of an effect called *refraction*. Light coming from the wire above the water goes straight into your eyes, but light from under the water changes direction when it goes through the glass and into the air. This makes the wire appear to be in a different place than it really is.

As the light changes direction through the water, the wire appears to bend

1 Make a "magic potion" by adding a few drops of food coloring to the glass of water. Don't make the color too dark because you need to see the wire through it.

2 Ask an adult to help you cut a piece of thin wire about 12 in. (30 cm) long with a pair of pliers. You could use part of a very thin wire coat hanger.

INTRODUCING MAGIC MIRIAM
AND THE
UNDERWATER CANDLE

Magic Miriam defies the laws of science to make a candle burn underwater!

Light the candle, open the side of the box and slide the candle into position (mark the right position before you start). The audience will be amazed to see something they've never seen before — a candle burning underwater.

WARNING: Be careful with fire. Make sure that the candle is not too near the box, and remember to blow it out after the trick.

WHAT YOU NEED
Clear plastic or glass
Cardboard box
Glass of water ★ Candle

THE SCIENCE BEHIND THE TRICK

The clear plastic or glass panel lets light from the glass of water through so that the audience can see it from the other side. Some of the light from the candle passes through the glass as well, but some is reflected back, making the candle appear to be inside the glass. In the past this effect was used to make ghosts appear on stage during plays — it's called "Pepper's ghost."

As light from the candle is reflected off the piece of glass, its image appears to hover in the glass of water

1 Paint the inside of the cardboard box black, and tape the box to a

base cut from the cardboard.

2 Fit the sheet of clear plastic or glass diagonally across the inside of the box.

3 Now cut a door in the front of the box, and decorate the box with symbols. Position the glass of water behind the glass partition, and mark the place where the candle should go in front of the partition.

INTRODUCING MAGIC MIRIAM
AND THE
MAGIC FLASHLIGHT

Magic Miriam stuns her audience with this illuminating trick!

For this trick you need a darkened room. Ask your assistant to turn off the lights. Cover the front of the flashlight with the red filter, and turn the flashlight on. Ask a volunteer to choose one of the coins and put it in the envelope. Pick up the envelope, which will look black. Turn off the flashlight. Swap the red filter for the green one, and turn on the flashlight to reveal the coin.

WHAT YOU NEED
Flashlight ★ Cardboard
Scissors ★ Glue ★ Coins
Red and green cellophane

THE SCIENCE
BEHIND THE TRICK

The light that comes out of a flashlight is called white light. It is made up of many different colors of light. The cellophane lets through only the red or green parts of the white light. It stops all the other colors. When red light shines on the green cellophane, it is prevented from passing through, so the cellophane looks black. Since the green light can go through, the coin can be seen.

Red light can't pass through the green cellophane

As green light passes through the green filter, the coin appears

1 Measure across the front of your flashlight. Make four identical frames from the cardboard, each large enough to fit over the

2 Make an envelope out of green cellophane. You should be able to put a coin in it and close it.

front of the flashlight. Cut squares of red and green cellophane and glue two frames onto each square, one on each side, to make a red and a green filter.

INTRODUCING MAGIC MARVIN
AND THE
CRAZY COLOR WHEEL

Magic Marvin's magic wheel mixes the rainbow colors to conjure up white.

WHAT YOU NEED
Cardboard box ★ Paints and colored paper Scissors ★ Thick and thin cardboard ★ Wooden dowels ★ Plastic lid

Put the box on your magic table with the color wheel facing the audience. In your patter, ask the audience to name all the colors on the wheel. Now announce that you will turn them all to white. Wave your magic wand, spin the handle faster and faster, and the colors will eventually appear white. Stop the wheel to get the colors back.

THE SCIENCE BEHIND THE TRICK

The light that comes from the Sun is white light. It's made up of many different colors, called the colors of the spectrum. When the wheel spins, your eyes are fooled into mixing the colors back into white.

GETTING PREPARED

1 Paint and decorate the cardboard box. Make small holes in the ends for a dowel.

2 Make a crank from a piece of thick cardboard and two dowels. Put the long dowel through the box, attaching the short rod and a handle to one end and the plastic lid to the other.

3 Now make a color wheel from the thin cardboard large enough to fit inside the plastic lid. Paint seven equal segments in the

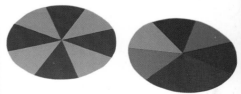

colors of the spectrum, or try mixing other colors.

25

INTRODUCING MAGIC MIRIAM
AND THE
TRANSPORTING BOX

It's incredible! How can the watch be in two places at the same time?

Place the two boxes on the table side by side, with the open sides facing each other. Both flaps should be closed. Ask a member of your audience to lend you a watch (a large one is best). Put the watch into the box without the mirror. Open the flap and check that the audience can see the watch. Now close that flap and open the flap on the other box. The watch has moved!

WHAT YOU NEED
Thick cardboard
Scissors ★ Cellophane tape ★ Small mirror
Colored paper or paints

THE SCIENCE
BEHIND THE TRICK

The transporting box works by reflection. The mirror in the second box reflects light from the watch out through the tube. This makes it look as though the watch is actually in the second box. If you look closely, you can see that the figures on the watch face are backward in the second box, so don't let anyone get too close!

An image of the watch is reflected into the second box and out through the door

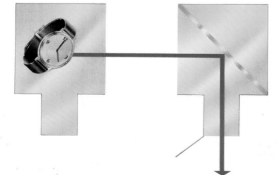

1 Make a cube-shaped box from the thick cardboard, with one side missing. The mirror should fit diagonally inside, as shown on page 26. Cut square holes in the top and front of the box. Make a square tube to fit on the front hole, and add a flap at the end.

2 Make another box, similar to the first, but with the opposite side missing. Decorate both boxes. The tubes should be exactly the same height.

HINTS AND TIPS

Here are some hints and tips for making your props. Good props will make your act look more professional, so spend time making and decorating your props, and look after them carefully. As well as the special props you need for each trick, try to make some general props such as a vest and a magic wand.

Decorate your props with magic shapes cut from colored paper. Paint bottles and tubes with oil-based paint.

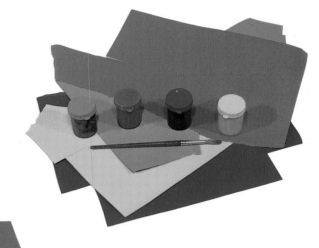

You will need cellophane tape and glue to make props. Double-sided tape may also be useful. Thick fabric-based tape is good for joining the edges of boxes together, and it's easy to paint too.

Stenciling is a good way to decorate large areas. Cut magic shapes such as stars and crescent moons out of cardboard. Throw away the shape, but keep the hole! Put the hole over the surface and paint through it with a sponge.

Your act will look more professional if you make a stage setting. This is easy if you have a backdrop to hang behind the stage. A large piece of black cloth is most effective. Using silver paint, stencil on stars and moons. The overall effect will be dramatic, creating an atmosphere of mystery and magic.

Make your own magician's clothes. Try to find an old hat and vest to decorate. If you can find some silvery material, cut out stars and moons and sew them on. An alternative is to use sequins or anything else that is shiny and dramatic so you look professional.

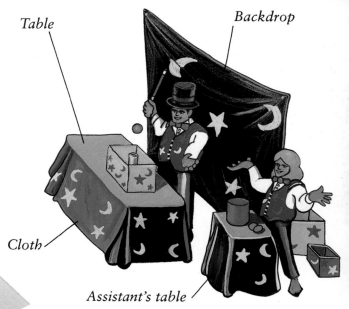

Table

Backdrop

Cloth

Assistant's table

Make a magician's table by draping a cloth over an ordinary table. Put the props out of sight underneath.

GLOSSARY

FILTER A colored piece of see-through paper that allows certain colors of light to pass through, but not others.

IMAGE The picture of an object that is produced by a lens or mirror. In the image, the parts are reversely arranged.

LIGHT A type of wave that can be seen by the eye. Also called visible light.

LINEAR PERSPECTIVE An optical illusion that makes parallel lines appear to meet in the distance.

REFLECTION The bouncing back of light from a surface.

REFRACTION The bending of light when it passes from one transparent substance to another.

MIRROR A piece of shiny glass that can reflect light to form an image.

OPTICAL ILLUSION The result of tricking the eye into seeing something that does not really exist.

SPECTRUM The band of rainbow colors that mix together to form "white light."

INDEX